AGILE PROJECT MANAGEMENT

Navigating Complexity with Efficiency and Adaptability (2023 Guide for Beginners)

Zachary Clark

Contents

1

What Exactly Is Agile Project Management?

Agile project management is a method of managing projects. Project administration. In a nutshell, it is a method of managing a project to help it achieve its objectives. This might involve completing a job ahead of schedule and continuously improving project procedures and products. Aside from that, agile project management focuses on developing a flexible scope and ensuring that products are tested to reflect a customer's various needs.

Everyone recognizes that a project takes complete focus, time, and careful preparation. Without these elements, it is impossible for a project to succeed. Every software project has a goal. Furthermore, each project has a completion date. Agile project management employs a variety of strategies to enhance project management. As a project leader, it is critical to keep current on agile project management practices. It is also beneficial to grasp the history of project management and the typical challenges that may arise.

The Beginning of Modern Project Management

From the creation of the printing press through the construction of the Great Wall of China, projects have existed.
Projects of all sizes have been present.

Project management, on the other hand, began around the middle of the twentieth century. Most scholars were searching for substantial advances and changes in the computer sector at this time. In order for these researchers to make these breakthroughs, they sought to establish efficient methods for managing and completing projects. Because these mechanisms were initially based on a systematic procedure, people in the fields of programming and computing adopted the majority of these processes.

One reason for this is that all computers were mostly hardware-based. The program was designed to grow. In reality, at the time, software was just a minor component of the computer. Remember that there was a time when computers were developed with thousands of physical tubes and just a few lines of code? As a result, the manufacturing technique used during this time period resulted in the creation of the waterfall approach.

Why should you go agile?
Now that you have a fundamental grasp of agile, you should also understand how it works, its responsibilities, and why you should use it.

Initially, we described agile project management as a method of project management that focuses on providing value to clients and the organization. In other words, this enables project managers to provide high-priority, high-quality work on a variety of projects.

Agile project management is a dynamic approach to project management that allows for any form of change that may occur. Agile project management will welcome the change, even late in the development process.

It will enable you to design the greatest features with the greatest value. With agile project management, you can be guaranteed to deal with real-time information while also managing scope, time, and cost.

The most intriguing aspect of project management using agile practices is how straightforward and efficient it is. It will help minimize complexity by reducing the time required to put together requirements for the whole project. It will also assist in developing the whole project and testing it in order to find different product faults.

Why should you be concerned about agile project management?
Let's imagine you've begun using agile practices and are finding it difficult; chances are, some things aren't working well. Perhaps some parts are missing. It is recommended in this instance to check the implementation procedure.

What everyone must understand is that executing Agile correctly will always result in delivery success.

In general, there must be a positive improvement in both the value provided to consumers and the product.

Time and cost are critical considerations in agile project management. It is constantly scrutinizing these two aspects, which are critical to every software project. Furthermore, it provides the team with immediate feedback. It also assists the team in adapting and implementing QA practices. This will aid in providing excellent service and results. Agile project managers focus on real-time delivery, proactive planning, and aggregate flow. The main objective is to keep project costs low while still delivering a workable product on schedule.

Agile project management software examples
Monday
Monday was formerly known as DaPulse. It primarily focuses on social communication and internal information exchange.

Monday has prioritised the best agile project management options. A board outlines who is working on what within a specified time frame to achieve collaboration. Then, teams can move on to comment on other team members' work or add necessary files. Real-time notification is made possible via a mobile or desktop application. Monday is excellent software for both basic and corporate plans.
Wrike

It is project management and collaboration software delivered as a service. Wrike is built with a simple user interface in mind. It has a project management function that helps you keep track of deadlines, project dependencies, and assignments and resources. To hold project data, it has an interactive Gantt chart, a sortable table, and a workload view that can be customised. Wrike's collaboration capabilities aid team members in talks, decision-making, and asset creation. These include Wrike's live co-editor, tools for attaching documents, tracking changes, and creating discussion threads. Wrike offers an "inbox" tool and browser notification to remind users of pending task changes from their dashboards. It is accessible through both iOS and native Android applications.

Asana

this is web-based software that is intended to improve cooperation. It primarily enables users to manage projects and online chores without using email. In a straightforward manner, Asana facilitates team collaboration, organisation, planning, and tracking of each member's progress.

Taiga

this open-source Agile Project Management platform is intended for smaller teams of project managers, developers, and designers. It makes project collaboration, time monitoring, and task management easier. Taiga has agile capabilities such as Kanban boards and backlogs that may be customised. This programme allows for web-based installations that are compatible with a wide range of operating systems. The system is available as a free, self-hosted model with public projects. There is also a premium plan with private projects.

Planbox

this enables people from many business departments to interact, plan, and develop agile initiatives. It uses the Scrum technique, which includes iterations, Scrum roles, a backlog, sprints, and story points. Planbox features a four-tiered platform with tasks, projects, initiatives, and items. Among other things, it enables drag-and-drop prioritisation, to-do lists, messaging, issue tracking, and reporting.

Smartsheet

Another SaaS-based tool that facilitates collaboration and job management Smartsheet uses a spreadsheet-like interface to organise projects, manage calendars, measure progress, and handle other tasks. Each entry in the smartsheet may have files connected to it, a discussion board linked to it, and emails saved. While information is being updated, another Smartsheet that is monitoring the same task is automatically updated.

Trello

It is a well-known brand of web-based project management software. A free account allows anyone to utilise the bulk of the capabilities, but a premium account offers more advanced features. Trello's design is based on the Kanban approach. Projects are seen as lists on a board. Each list has a progressive card with drag-and-drop capabilities.

2

Agile Project Management Implementation

An agile project was defined in the previous chapter.

Management. Remember that agile project management is an iterative process that takes user input into account, adjusts to changes, and creates a workable outcome.

This chapter will look at how to put agile project management into practise. This chapter is very useful for project managers who wish to understand how to implement agile practises in their organisations.

Let us first examine agile project management in depth:

Agile is a practise that is iterated upon. This indicates that it is used in tiny doses. Based on earlier input, each chunk has been improved.

Agile is characterised as both a method and an attitude. It is not a set of instructions. In reality, seeing Agile as a black-and-white template is a mistake.

After each iteration, Agile produces a practical working result. This entails developing a preliminary draught and updating it in response to customer comments.

Agile project management entails efficiently communicating through a series of emails or meetings. It entails effectively communicating in a proper and accurate manner.

Agile practises provide rapid development, increased income, and increased release frequency. So, why not use agile project management for your organisation or team? When using Agile to build projects, you don't just throw in your documentation, tools, and plans. Even if they are crucial, the primary factors to consider are iteration, cooperation, and prototypes.

Most users are not concerned with documentation or long-term planning. Instead, they expect anything they desire to be supplied promptly. A majority would prefer that an issue be resolved immediately rather than waiting one month.

Users have a lot of requirements these days, and there is no better way to meet those expectations than with agile.

How can you identify whether agile is right for your team?

Agile is a fantastic method to construct projects; however, not every project can reap the full advantages of Agile practises.

Agile reimagines an organisation's working methods. It alters everything from the moment a team of developers starts working on a project until the moment the project requirements are established. It shortens the time it takes to complete a job. As a result, all project managers must determine if their organisation is prepared to handle all of the changes that agile project management brings to the project cycle. To be sure, here are a few questions to think about:

Are you willing to start a project without knowing where it will end?

Agile project management entails finishing tiny pieces of a project in a short amount of time. A product is tested in real time with consumers, and comments regarding the product are recorded. It might be unpleasant and exhausting for someone who is not accustomed to this sort of procedure. As a result, it is critical that everyone on the team is prepared and comfortable with delivering a half-baked product to test with users before the organisation chooses whether or not to implement agile development practises.

What are your risk tolerance levels?

A key feature of agile projects is the continual delivery of a product and the learning from faults identified by consumers. For individuals who are not accustomed to taking chances, this may be a high-risk endeavour.

The willingness to take a huge risk and start an organisational transformation is a big choice. So, before fully implementing Agile practises, it is critical to be prepared to deal with any unfamiliar challenges that may arise.

Determine your team's degree of adaptability.

When it comes to developing agile products, it is necessary to collaborate directly with clients in order to enhance the product. It is not like how developers and designers create products based on their perceptions of what a product should be. Instead, the product is developed in response to client input.

How does the organisation's structure affect discipline?

One of the most important aspects of Agile is the collaboration between developers and the primary stakeholders. This is not always simple in certain businesses. In reality, some have a convoluted hierarchy that makes it difficult to communicate with stakeholders. Consider the kind of hierarchy that exists in your organisation.

What methods do you use to assess success and progress?

Agile emphasises constant labour to improve and develop a product. As a consequence, someone who is quick to embrace a new concept and discard the prior one may not obtain the optimum outcomes from Agile. To assist in reaching the objectives specified, it is critical to take the time to redefine the measurements of success or development.

Agile implementation

Project managers are responsible for ensuring that everyone works properly. They must ensure that a team remains focused on the needs specified by the customer. Project managers have an easier time overseeing a project while using Agile. The seven phases of implementing Agile in an organisation are outlined below.

Step 1: Create a vision.

What exactly is it?

A clear vision of the project must be developed at the outset of an agile project. This implies that the project manager and team meet to identify the project's reference ground. An elevator pitch is a great technique for a product firm to learn about a project's concept.

Companies that are developing anything other than a product, on the other hand, must alter their pitch and develop tactics that meet the demands of the organisation.

Who should be there?

At this stage, one must identify potential customers for the product. It is recommended that key stakeholders such as managers, product owners, and corporate directors be invited.

When should it occur?

It is critical that a strategy meeting take place prior to the commencement of every project in order to keep the project's purpose alive.

How long should it continue?

While it is up to you, a good strategy meeting should last between 4 and 16 hours, with breaks in between.

Step 2: Make a plan for your product.

What exactly is it?

Once the strategy has been approved, the product owner should turn it into a product roadmap.

This is a sophisticated picture of the project's needs, with a flexible schedule for when each project should be created.

The "flexible" timescale is crucial here since you can't prepare for each step for a month. As a result, each product element should be prioritised, identified, and given an approximate cost. This will make it easier to supply a ready-to-use product.

Items that must be present

the product owner's duty is to design the product roadmap, but it should also have buy-in and involvement from other stakeholders involved in the project.

When should it happen?

Before planning sprints, ensure that a roadmap is in place. As a result, it is preferable to begin developing a product after the strategy discussion has concluded.

How long should that continue?

Agile project management necessitates quick product development. There should be no delays in the planning phases. However, the product roadmap is the product's mission, and it must last until the product owner feels that everything has been covered.

Step 3: Prepare with a published plan.

What exactly is it?

So far, there is already a strategy in place as well as a timetable. At this stage, it is the product owner's responsibility to develop an advanced timetable that would outline the successive release dates of the functional programme. Remember that agile projects have several product releases before the final product is launched. As a result, a product owner has the choice of emphasising the product characteristics that he or she wants to market first. For example, if a project began in November, it may be scheduled to be released in February, then again in May when the most advanced features have been built. However, this is dependent on the project's complexity and the length of the sprints.

Who should be there?

On the day of the product launch, the top members of the organisation should be present. Team members and supervisors should also be present. A few stakeholders will also help energise the team.

When should it occur?

It is important to guarantee that a functional product is released on the specified date.

How much time should it take?

Be honest with yourself about the duration of a session. Take care not to let it slow things down. An interval of 4–8 hours should be enough

Step 4: Schedule your sprints.
What exactly is it?
This is the time to switch from a macro to a micro perspective. Make sure the sprints are brief and focused on a particular goal. You may configure the sprint to last 1-4 weeks and keep the duration consistent throughout the project to help teams prepare accurately.

When beginning a sprint cycle, ensure that a team creates a list that includes a backlog of items to complete within a specified timeframe. This will aid in the delivery of working software.

Who must be present?
This is the team's common obligation. In other words, the project manager, product owner, and team members should all be present to provide feedback on the product.

When should it happen?
Sprint planning is always done at the start of each sprint cycle.

How long should it continue?
Remember that preparing a sprint sets the tone for the cycle; yet, you don't want to spend too much time at this point. It should last between 2 and 4 hours. In addition, after the sprints are planned, the team may begin.

Step 5: Check that your team is on track.
There must be time set aside during the sprint creation process to deal with any difficulties that arise.

Many of these challenges can lengthen the time it takes to achieve the goals. As a result, a project manager should schedule daily meetings with their team. Meetings may take up to 15 minutes.

The meeting will cover the following topics:

- what did the team accomplish the day before?
- Current projects being worked on by the team;
- Challenges that the team has faced

Although this may appear to some team members to be a waste of time, holding such meetings helps clarify certain points in the meeting. Remember that agile practises require a rapid reaction to challenges, and exposing these issues in public is the best way to foster team cooperation.

Step 6: You've completed sprints. It's time to take a look back.
What exactly is it?

Assume that everything has gone according to plan. As a result, functioning software should be available to deliver before the conclusion of each sprint cycle. This is the time for the team to go through everything before presenting it to the stakeholders and any visitors in attendance.

The best way is to go through the original plan and ensure that all of the criteria have been satisfied. It is up to you, as the product owner, to determine whether or not particular functionalities should be deleted. If you are dissatisfied with a specific functionality, you have the right to challenge it. Determine how they may change their working tempo so that they can meet the following round's objectives.

Who should be there?

During each sprint review, the entire project team, as well as stakeholders, must be present. After seeing the product, each participant group must provide comments.

When should it occur?

A sprint review should take place at the conclusion of each sprint. This should just take an hour or two.

Step 7: What happens next? Choose what you want to concentrate on during your next sprint.
What exactly is it?

For agile project management to function well, a template or rough sketch of what should be done next must be accessible. This should be specified in the next sprint. When a sprint is finished, it is time to plan out activities and tasks for the next round. To help identify what should be done in the next sprint, it is necessary to evaluate the previous sprint's suggestions and work out how to incorporate them into the next one.

Who should be there?

Project stakeholders, directors, and team members should all be present.

When should this occur?

It is ideal if a sprint retrospective takes place immediately after a sprint review.

How long should this last?

Make it brief and engaging. One to two hours is enough time to evaluate the current sprint and plan the next one.

So, what should happen next?

At this point, it is critical to deploy operational software so that consumers may examine it and provide comments. This is an excellent time to consider adding new features. The never-ending shipping, creating, and learning is a crucial element that makes Agile the ideal practise to employ.

Agile encourages the delivery of a half-baked product and allows people to provide input on the product. This implies that a missing capability may be identified before a product's final release.

3

Agile vs. Waterfall Model

S mart project management has become an essential tool for firms today. Excellent project Management is the reason why organizations work smoothly and without problems in their procedures.

So far, every business, large or small, has used technology and better project management tools to ensure that it builds and delivers the correct software.

The adoption of these technologies has improved the software development process, regardless of whether it involves team cooperation. In fact, it has made things function smoothly and efficiently.

Although there are numerous approaches to project management, the most outstanding approach is agile project management because it is flexible and practical. Agile practises offer individuals the ability to accomplish a variety of activities. This is one of the reasons for its popularity. The following are some of the distinctions between Agile and the conventional method:

Traditional Agile

Traditional project management should be defined

Much has been said about agile project management and how beneficial it is for project managers to employ it in the software development process. To appreciate how excellent it is, though, one must first grasp how conventional project management works.

The waterfall model is another name for the conventional technique. This name was chosen because of its form. This method implies a linear pattern in which each step of the operation happens in order. The waterfall model is based on predictability. Predictability relates to the ability to foresee experience and the tools employed. Every project follows the same life cycle. Planning, designing, testing, feasibility, and production support are all steps involved.

The waterfall technique involves early preparation with no scope to change the project's needs. The emphasis in this strategy is on time and money, but the project criteria remain the same. This is one of the reasons why initiatives based on the waterfall approach face financial and timing constraints. The table below summarises the distinctions between agile and conventional project management.

Features Agile as it has always been done

Project Size: Large-scale Small and medium-sized scale

User specifications Before any implementation, fully defined

input that is interactive

Organisational structure

Iterative Linear Client Participation Process of Low to High Development

Life cycle analysis An iterative delivery procedure

The expense of resuming

High to low

Developmental model

After coding, dynamic testing was completed. Every iteration

Requirements At the start, everything was standard and well-known. Changes occur quickly.

Architecture produces current and predictable needs.

Produces current needs

Why do we favor agile over the waterfall method?

Many developers and project managers prefer agile methodologies. Let us look at some of those reasons:

• Project difficulty

Agile

If a company wants to solve a complex project, this is the methodology to use. An advanced project may have many phases that are linked together, and each stage may rely on other stages rather than just one. This is why most project managers choose to employ Agile for large and complex projects.

Traditional

the conventional technique may be appropriate for modest projects with few complicated aspects. However, one must recognise that unexpected changes in the project or certain complexities may affect the entire process and force one to return to step one.

• Flexibility

Agile

Agile is popular because of the agility it provides in project development. Complicated undertakings have numerous phases that are interdependent. Because agile methodology allows for adaptability, one can take a risk and change something at any stage.

Traditional

the waterfall technique is based on the idea that once a step is completed, there is no turning back. In summary, the conventional method lacks flexibility. If a client requests that changes be made immediately, it becomes difficult to change. The only choice is to return to the initial step. This may be a huge waste of time.

• **The scope of input received changes.**

Agile

Agile methodology is the finest in the industry for gathering input on a specific software product.

This is due to the fact that it has a flexible procedure that welcomes comments after a product is delivered to consumers. Feedback aids in the improvement of a product as well as the resolution of any problems. The Agile methodology's flexibility is the primary reason why most organisational managers opt to utilise it. Because they deal with small tasks in a large project, software developers who use this methodology can respond quickly to customer requests.

Traditional

Before beginning implementation under the waterfall paradigm, each step is thoroughly described. This method cannot handle rapid changes or input that may require swift reactions. The conventional strategy has a set time and budget in most circumstances.

Agile project development characteristics

Divides the project into smaller components

Agile divides a project into smaller parts known as iterations. The iteration is then delivered to the client for evaluation. The success of an agile project is determined by what is accomplished after each iteration.

Self-organized

there is a parallel management paradigm in agile development. This is when firm personnel are supervised by a group rather than a single individual. Agile projects are often divided into three parts:

- the product's owner
- The scrum master

The team

Customer involvement

When it comes to agile development, the client comes first. The consumer is crucial to the development of each iteration. The customer's responsibility is to examine the iteration and give feedback. Once the feedback is received, the appropriate action is taken.

Overall, Agile is the project management system leader. When compared to other approaches, Agile's characteristics stand out. That is why it is the most widely used software project management approach.

4

Learn more about Scrum and Agile Principles

Scrum and Agile are words used often in the area of engineering. They are phrases used by technical engineers. It's almost as if it's a part of their language. However, for those who are unfamiliar with the language, it can be frustrating.

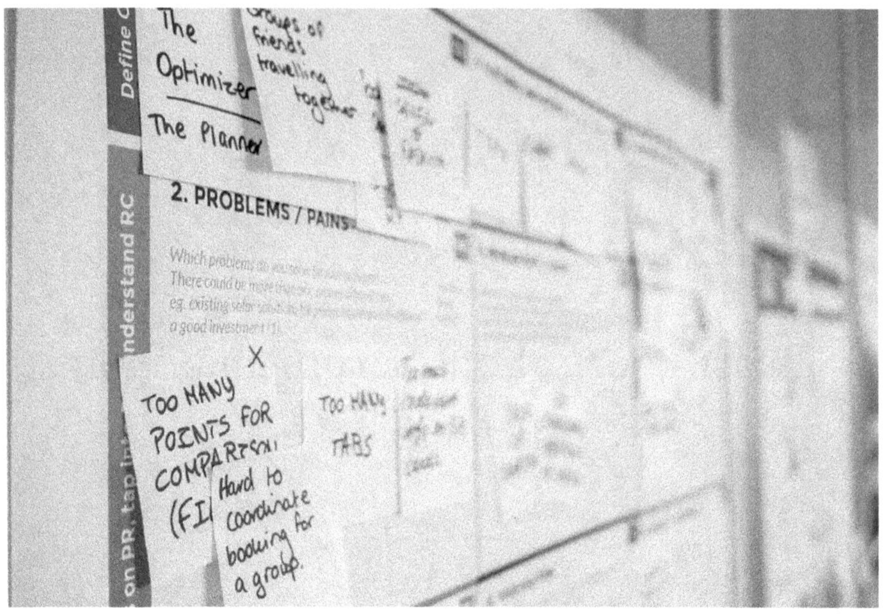

What is the difference between Scrum and Agile?

When you first start using Scrum and Agile, things may not be simple. Anyone can be perplexed by these two words because they can be used interchangeably.

But don't be confused because the two words have different meanings.

So far, you've figured out what agile means. There is no need to describe it here. How about a scrum?

In short, Scrum is an agile development framework. The distinction between Scrum and Agile may be shown by comparing a diet to a recipe.

A vegetarian follows a diet that is based on certain practises and ideas. The basis for developing a vegetarian diet is a recipe for preparing vegetables. This example attempts to demonstrate the relationship between Agile and Scrum.

Who may profit from the use of Scrum?

It is incorrect to believe that Scrum was designed just for engineers and developers. In reality, this framework may be used to create any other kind of project. Scrum may be used in any sort of project, whether it is in the market or any other area. Scrum is the ideal framework for gathering ideas and organising a project team.

Scrum's Components

to understand how Scrum works, one must first grasp the framework's components and the individuals involved. The greatest part is that no prior experience is required.

There is no prerequisite expertise required to begin using Scrum. The sole need is a location to help generate thoughts. A whiteboard or software like Trello might be used. Scrum's components are listed below.

Product Manager. This is the individual who represents the user's best interests and can express what he or she wants to see in the final product. The backlog is created by the product owner. A "backlog" is a list of needs or tasks for the finished product.Sprint. This is the time range in which a team is expected to execute many tasks.Scrum on a daily basis. This relates to the daily updates provided by the teams.

Retrospective.

This should help you see that Scrum is relatively simple to understand since no extra tools are required. The only key is to learn the jargon and follow the rules.

Scrum Framework Fundamentals

keep in mind that no prior experience or specific training is necessary to begin utilising Scrum. You can educate yourself. The fundamentals of Scrum are simple to grasp. The most difficult element is mastering the skills. Scrum experts think that although one may understand the rules of Scrum in 10 minutes, becoming an expert in Scrum takes years.

The Agile Principles

A project may be managed using one of 12 key concepts. These concepts are most effective when used in conjunction with Scrum.

Customer satisfaction is the primary aim, which is achieved by the continual and quick supply of a product or software.

Changing settings or conditions is welcomed at any step in the process in order to provide the greatest result to the consumer.

A service or product is supplied more often.

Every day, stakeholders and developers collaborate.

To get the greatest outcomes from the project, both stakeholders and team members must stay motivated.

Physical meetings are the best way to learn about the status of a project.

The overall success metric is a finished, functioning product.

Sustainable development is achieved via an agile methodology in which both stakeholders and the development team can keep a consistent pace.

Agility is achieved by a subsequent emphasis on technological quality and proper design.

The importance of simplicity cannot be overstated.

A self-organising team primarily generates the appropriate architecture and designs to meet the requirements.

Regular meetings help improve productivity and refine products.

The Best Scrum Master Skills to Help Steer Digital Innovation in the Company

A scrum master is an essential part of the Agile methodology. This individual is in charge of guiding the team in implementing best practises and removing barriers.

Although there is a "master," these people are not masters. They are servant leaders who assist the product owner and the service team. This implies that a total shift in thinking will be required. The capacity to adjust and continually be ready to develop yourself and your team members are the top scrum master abilities that everyone should have to help move digital innovation further.

Master these three Scrum Master abilities to become a Scrum Hero.
Listen

Typically, Type a personalities enjoy taking charge and directing others on what they should do. There may be instances when you feel the need to get up and provide commands in order for things to go smoothly. For example, you may be the first to speak and provide guidance during scrum meetings. Maybe you already know the right way to do things, and sometimes you simply know.

However, the focus of agile development is on the team achieving a common goal and delivering the end product.

The main goal is to get the team to operate as effectively and efficiently as possible. It is difficult to achieve your objective if you are unable to listen to and learn from your team members. It is vital to listen to some of the difficulties that the team comes up with, the ideas they make, and the changes they would want to implement.

How to effectively listen

most people aren't natural listeners, so the best way to begin is to act like one. Make sure you don't speak until the other person has finished speaking. Avoid interrupting someone who is speaking. Second, avoid quietly debating with them in your brain or planning how you will answer. Finally, try to repeat whatever they said to ensure that you comprehend everything they intended to say. Every day, practise your listening skills with a one-on-one chat before moving on to scrum meetings.

Coach

The most crucial component of the agile process is the team you lead and direct. As a result, it is your obligation to guarantee that each member of the team learns and develops. If you see a developer suffering, don't push it under the rug. Come out and assist them. Help them attain their goals by guiding them through each obstacle with recommendations. Take advantage of one-on-one time throughout the meeting. This teaching method has been proven to be beneficial at the outset of a project. It will also assist in avoiding complications that may develop later in the project. If you discover a team member who is generating problems, confront them as soon as possible. Do not be frightened or hesitant about discussing it. Remember. A little issue overlooked now may become a major one tomorrow.

How can I teach people most effectively?

Coaching's purpose is to provide feedback to team members and individuals. Repeat as many times as you can.

Is it the work of a single developer or the whole team?

Praise them privately or publicly, based on their personality features. Do you see anything that a person might improve? Inform the members of your feelings. Begin by explaining what went wrong and making innovative recommendations for how to fix it. When you learn to provide suggestions or feedback on a consistent basis, team members will come to expect and appreciate it. As feedback becomes routine, team members will begin to take it personally or even avoid it.

Facilitate

A scrum master's objectives include meeting facilitation and coaching on best practises. This indicates that you are not permitted to tell others what they should do. In every meeting, the team should work together. The finest facilitators are those who are so inconspicuous that no one recognises they are there.

How can I help the most effectively?

Good listening skills are essential for successful facilitators. They ask fantastic questions to help them comprehend everyone's point of view and guide the group along. Good facilitators stay impartial and do not favour any particular viewpoint. They are self-assured and believe in themselves. They believe that by working together, they will be able to reach an agreement and find answers. It is critical to understand that no one is born a facilitator, and hence anybody may learn how to be an excellent facilitator.

To summarise, a scrum master must be a diligent worker. Furthermore, it is always encouraging to see a team work together to achieve results more quickly.

Although the aforementioned skills are important for scrum masters, everyone has the responsibility to facilitate, listen, and assist others.

5

Making Your Company Agile

The main challenge is how to transform a whole organization into an agile one. Typically, in a properly developed organization, The manager's responsibility in agile practices is to guarantee that all members stay dedicated to their tasks and abilities. When every team member is committed to their job, the customer receives more value. Furthermore, the manager must have complete confidence in the actions of those in contact with the customer. The manager should also have faith in his or her staff to perform things correctly. Agile is neither a top-down nor a bottom-up method. The primary emphasis is on providing the right value to consumers. In other words, the client, not the management, is in charge.

The manager in the conventional model, on the other hand, has a different duty than the manager in the agile technique. In this model, the manager's responsibility is to identify what needs to be done and to advise staff on how to accomplish it. Furthermore, managers ensure that the employee completes the work in accordance with all of the instructions.

This paradigm implies that the employee's responsibility is to follow instructions and trust the manager's judgments.

The primary purpose of this approach is to produce revenue for the company.

As a result, the manager is the boss.

The manager is the boss in many organizations.

As a result, implementing agile practices is difficult.

Any efforts made are thwarted due to ongoing conflict between the managers and the agile team. As a result, allowing team members to embrace agile practices in these types of organizations becomes tough. It will most likely never be realized.

Why are partial solutions not the best solution?

Many organizations have reported conflict between management and the adoption of agile practices. To alleviate this conflict, it is critical to modify the role of the agile team leader to match that of an agile approach. This is accomplished by writing a new job description for the project manager. However, this approach only provides a short-term solution. The following are some of the reasons why it is not permanent:

There are several management levels in a large organization. Because the manager's job description was redefined, the friction between the agile team and the top hierarchy was only reduced by one layer. When the highest managers in the hierarchy continue to accept conventional leadership, it is very difficult for the friction to cease.

Another source of impending conflict is that senior executives in large corporations have just one goal: to make money for the company's shareholders and executives. This strategy is known as "maximizing shareholder value. A strategy that is not in line with the goals of agile methodology. Remember that the goal of agile initiatives is to provide value to the client. The generation of money is a byproduct of agile practices, but it is not their primary purpose.

As a result, until a lasting solution is discovered, implementing agility in these organizations will always be tough.

Why do the top executives detest Agile?

Is it feasible for an organization's senior management to adopt Agile without first debating the organization's goals? No, it does not. Top managers use a command-and-control strategy to generate enormous profits and raise the stock price. The best way is to resolve the conflict between an agile team and senior management.

The most effective method is the economics of creativity.

Top firms like Apple, Zara, and Google do things differently. These businesses take advantage of the creative economy. As a result, they have redefined the organization's objective and switched the emphasis from shareholders to customers. Top leaders in these firms appreciate customer value. In a nutshell, they are agile-friendly.

Money is the ultimate product of their agile practices, but it is not their primary purpose. The main objective is to please the consumer. Google and Apple are excellent examples of how an agile approach has produced financial outcomes.

It is quite difficult to overcome the conflict between agile and conventional management in a sensible manner.

It is difficult because the conventional position of management includes deeply ingrained attitudes, beliefs, and ideals about how the world works. This adds to the business culture. Previous experience has shown that altering the business culture through approaches, choices, and descriptions may be difficult.

However, managers must stop displaying a boss mentality and begin to embrace agility. Through experience, one must reach out to managers on a deeper emotional level. This has the potential to lead managers to accept differing attitudes, beliefs, and understandings of how the world works. The manager should cultivate a favorable relationship with the consumer.

Most of the time, this is difficult to understand since the job of a manager seems to be permanently etched in the culture of the organization. This culture includes safeguarding a set of practices, objectives, and values. This implies that, although a manager may prefer to avoid acting like a boss and instead focus on the client, the current culture makes change difficult.

Small aspects of a culture are combined to thwart any attempts to change it. Individual individuals may attempt to modify it, but it will be difficult due to other factors in the organization. It is vital to understand that this is not a home where one can rebuild one area and leave the rest alone. No. An organization is like a series of interlocking patterns. To transition to Agile, five fundamental changes must be made: Instead of focusing on making money for the organization, the primary goal should be to please the client. The job should be done in a self-organizing team rather than having individuals who do the task report to the managers. Furthermore, management should ensure that it does not check to see if those who are supposed to perform a given task have done so. It should strive to make the work easier for the people who will be doing it.

Allow agile principles to guide work completion rather than bureaucratic guidelines, reports, and plans.

Rather than being preoccupied with predictability and efficiency, the primary values should be constant development and transparency.

The replacement of a one-way top-down directive with a horizontal discourse Organizational culture transformation

by deciding to use these five solutions to help deploy Agile in a different organization, the business culture gains a new image. Remember that this is not an easy task. It necessitates the integration of business resources.

Overall, the most effective technique for achieving success is to begin with leadership tools.Control systems, a vision of the future, and power tools are examples of such tools.

Leadership's Importance in Storytelling

The ability to tell a good tale is essential for changing business cultures all around the globe. Leadership storytelling is about more than simply getting something done. It is the correct path for leaders to take in order to embrace change. Instead of pushing for change via propositional arguments, which may generate many debates, leaders have the potential to gain credibility through storytelling. Once they demonstrate a strong belief in these narratives, they spread and foster creativity, interaction, and transformation. Storytelling is an incredible tool for dealing with the difficulty of altering company culture. It transforms abstract figures into a visually appealing image. Keep in mind that every successful company has a story to tell.

6

Agile Principles and the Agile Manifesto

i t is just impossible to see how software and action may interact have developed as a result of "The Agile Manifesto." Prior to this "Manifesto," software development was a slow process.Because of a change in business requirements, many initiatives in the pipeline are often cancelled.

The Agile Manifesto is the main pillar of the agile movement. Beyond software development, the use of Agile has been achieved in manufacturing, collaboration, communication, and the rapid development of granular features under the control of the general plan.

History of the Agile Manifesto

This manifesto was written in response to difficulties in the 1990s. There was a significant delay between product delivery and requirement analysis. Many projects were cancelled as a result of this. It was during this time that company requirements and consumer requirements changed, resulting in a final product that did not meet current demands. The previous software development approaches were unable to meet the needs. Later that year, the Agile Manifesto and the 12 principles were published.

The Agile manifesto's values

the 'Agile Manifesto and the 12 principles that underlie it' include four important values. These concepts and ideals underpin all agile techniques. Participants and individuals managing tools and processes

it is the first of the Agile Manifesto's values. It focuses on people rather than technologies and procedures. This is because people are the ones who react to a company's requirements and move it along. If the tools or processes drive development, chances are the team will not actively engage in the improvements, which may lead to customer dissatisfaction. Working software versus extensive documentation

traditionally, a significant amount of effort was spent developing a document to be utilized in product development and delivery. Technical specifications, test plans, paperwork, and approvals were all necessary. This lengthy list caused software development to be delayed. Agile does not remove documentation, but it does provide a far better approach for developers to know what to do. Agile documents are developed as user stories that are sufficient to aid in software development. The Agile Manifesto values documentation, but it also values functional software considerably more.

Customer collaboration in contract negotiation

Negotiation refers to the meeting between a client and a product manager to finalize project specifics. Customers discuss in depth the needs of a product in the early phases of a software model such as the waterfall model. In this situation, the consumer participates in the development. They do not, however, contribute to the product's development. The Agile Manifesto offers a platform for customers to participate throughout the product development process. As a result, it is easy for the team to match the demands of the consumer. Agile approaches may engage the client at various stages of the demo, but they may also involve the end user in daily development. This ensures that all criteria are met.

4. Reaction to a modification in a future plan

Changes in software are seen as an added expense in conventional software development methodologies. As a consequence, it is resistant to change. The objective is to build a complete strategy with a variety of elements. All of the elements in this strategy are labeled with the highest priority.

There is also a high degree of reliance on a team to work on a problem. However, due to the short iteration length of agile methodology, it is possible to shift priorities from one iteration to the next. In addition, additional features are being included in the next generation.

As a result, Agile offers a constructive reaction to change. The method-tailoring approach is a prominent example. This technique involves humans selecting a system's growth strategy via various tweaks. Agile enables a team to modify the process and verify that it meets the demands of the user.

The 12 Principles of the Agile Manifesto

these ideas define a culture in which change is welcomed and the client is prioritized. These 12 principles are as follows:

Customer satisfaction is achieved by regular software releases. This implies that clients should be pleased when they observe the development of their projects rather than waiting for the release date.

Withstand changes in requirements during the development process.

Consistent delivery of functional software.

A collaboration between developers and company owners throughout the process.

Trust, support, and inspiration are provided to all parties involved.

Allow for face-to-face interactions.

Working software is the foundation for measuring progress.

Agile procedures enhance the subsequent development pace.

To boost agility, concentrate on technical specifications and design.

Provide simplicity. Create things in the proper manner to guarantee that everything functions well.

Better architectures, designs, and needs should be promoted via self-organizing organizations.

A follow-up meeting will be held to verify that the correct product has been developed.

Agile's goal is to ensure that both development and business requirements are met. Agile initiatives are customer-friendly and encourage customers to engage in the development process. As a result, Agile has proven to be a game changer in software development.

7

Agile Software Development Techniques

There has been a lot of discussion so far.

Agile and the reasons why business owners and executives should adopt agile development in their organization or firm there is also a lot of agile information on the internet. As a result, new participants who wish to embrace agile may be perplexed about what to do.

Agile is a fantastic technique for developing a product or software. It is a versatile method that supports anyone seeking success in software development and product creation. The following are crucial characteristics that should be present to ensure the success of agile techniques:

• A shared understanding of the process and objectives

- • commitment;

• Cooperation among all stakeholders

- • Openness
- • Willingness to exchange information

Techniques for Agile Software Development

Continuous Integration

This method involves team members collaborating on a product. Members then integrate their smaller developments with the rest of the team. Each integration is assessed to see whether there is an issue with the integration process. If a problem is discovered, appropriate action is taken to resolve it.

Development through testing

it is a coding method that repeats a brief development cycle several times. The first step for a developer is to design an automated test case that measures a new function. The new code is then refactored to accommodate new standards after producing a shortcode that passes a given test.

Programming in pairs

with this technique, two programmers work at the same station. The first is the programmer, and the second is the driver, whose job it is to go through each line of code submitted.

Patterns in Design

a reusable solution is an essential part of the design process in software engineering. A design pattern is incomplete unless and until it is turned into code. It is a method of solving a problem that may be used in a variety of scenarios. Patterns are formal practices that a programmer might use in his or her application.

Object-oriented patterns depict the linkages and interactions that exist between objects and classes. They accomplish this without defining the object types or apps that are used.

Design that is domain-driven

this technique's concept is as follows:

Align several complicated designs on a single model.

Make domain logic the major emphasis of the project.

Begin a process of creative cooperation between domain specialists and the technical team in order to lessen the conceptual heart issue.

Domain-driven approaches do not constitute a methodology. It basically gives a set of practices that aid in the design and acceleration of software projects dealing with complicated domains.

Refactoring of code

this is a method of altering the software system without compromising its outward characteristics. The most essential aspect of the adjustments is that they enhance the internal structure of the software system.

8

Challenges of Implementing Agile

Particularly for individuals who will be utilizing it for the first time. This chapter examines some of the difficulties that may arise with the implementation of Agile.

It is vital to remember that convincing a whole business to forsake the conventional paradigm and adopt agile principles takes time. However, once that is completed, there are numerous advantages to going agile. When implementing agile practices, the right tool to have is one that is complex and will aid in the implementation. Understand that Agile necessitates a few adjustments to corporate culture as well as a systemic change in the firm or organization.

Scrum seems to be a significant impediment to actual work

to be effective, a scrum master and all team members should have prior experience managing team projects. It will assist in dealing with situations such as delays and so on. Six months of experience is sufficient to address the majority of the challenges that emerge. A person with more than six months of experience, on the other hand, has a greater probability of dealing with all of the challenges. Great experience adds value and meaning to the development of agile initiatives. A person who has worked on multiple waterfall projects and experienced a great deal of displeasure with how projects are handled is the best match.

Without this sort of expertise, dealing with the scrum master may be difficult.

Remember that CSM training is insufficient, and the Scrum Master will not lead the team in making everyday choices. Scrum and Agile are practical frameworks that need careful consideration since each project is unique. As a result, experience is essential. Because of their limited exposure, most experienced developers say that Scrum and Agile are unproductive. Overall, a team that includes all necessary personnel is more likely to succeed in agile implementation.

Scrum may seem redundant to developers who are accustomed to working autonomously, and it may slow them down.

There is no doubt that Scrum adds some overhead to the development process when compared to alternative development techniques that lack a structured methodology. A scrum is a tool for managing agile projects. It aids in the generation of helpful insights in the management of project status.

Certain projects are better completed by a smaller group of developers who work independently. Consider the personal Kanban. This is an excellent project management tool for such tasks. However, if you want to narrow down to a team of product owners and developers, it is critical to clearly specify the team members' collaboration. Scrum is the ideal answer for this situation.

Whether you will employ a collaborative method or an individual-based strategy should depend entirely on the specifics of the project.Similarly, if a project relies on an existing solution and has subject matter experts present, a collaborative method like Scrum is recommended. Again, if the number of parties involved in communication exceeds three, the agile approach can be modified.

Some development efforts are not appropriate for a timed sprint

this is yet another issue. Normal-size prints do not employ certain sorts of development. Here is a partial list:

• A completely new and complicated user interface design

• A new architectural system

• Database ETL that requires transformation, cleansing, and so on.

Some of these may take several tries in order to get anything to function. They are all faced with the identical issue of complying with a set sprint-sized effort.

A sprint's goal is to enable testing and demonstrate that a backlog item works correctly. A sprint also aids in the development of appropriate functionality. Teamwork, discipline, and focus are essential to ensuring that no one misses the deadline for completing a sprint. One of the biggest issues is the phrase "to the end user." Certain development tasks may take longer if end users are defined as application consumers. However, there are some steps that can be taken to ensure that these tasks are completed using the appropriate agile framework. The three issue areas are listed below.

• **A brand-new architecture system:** This contains many physical components, software applications, numerous organizational IT levels, and administrative personnel. It is critical to purchase hardware, install it, and guarantee that it functions properly.

When applying for third-party hardware, the applicant must have access to in-house applications. Depending on the organization's current infrastructure, security should be upgraded.

• **Complex UI Design:** It may take many attempts to get it perfect. Both the development team and the SMEs should do several trial-and-error checks. The trials and mistakes should result in the publication of several mockups, wireframes, and graphics.

• **Database ETL:** This may need a number of layers to allow data cleansing, extraction, and transformation.

Finally, the data is displayed in accordance with the project specifications. A presentation enables the user to see the results of their labor.

9

Agile Methodology

Nowadays, most software companies adopt agile software development techniques in the most effective manner possible

They are capable. Whether it is the first time in the history of application development or not, most development approaches now rely on the agile methodology.

So, what exactly is agile methodology? How does it fit into software development? This chapter examines several agile approaches

Scrum

it is a widely utilized strategy in many businesses.

Scrum is an iterative technique that focuses on establishing the primary features and goals prior to a sprint. Scrum's goal is to decrease risk while adding value.

Scrum uses a narrative tool to outline how specific features should function and be evaluated. After that, the Scrum team proceeds through a series of sprints to provide modest provisions. To facilitate the effective functioning of a scrum team, it is important to address any issues that may develop early on.

Scrum differs from the waterfall model in that it is iterative and collaborative. The waterfall technique, for example, requires extensive documentation. This style of documentation makes it tough to modify features that may be inappropriate in a certain setting. When using Scrum methodology, developers and testers should collaborate on a regular basis through sprint retrospectives. These sessions guarantee good communication and emphasize any points that may be unclear. A scrum master will also be present at all times to monitor the progress of the project.

As a result of the rapid iterations, this technique is ideal for teams working on a project where consumers and stakeholders demand a functioning product be released as soon as possible.

This kind of collaboration assists the team in making any essential modifications that stakeholders or product owners may point out.

Kanban

Manufacturing is the emphasis of this agile technique.

Kanban may be thought of as having a long to-do list at its heart. The Kanban technique, like Scrum, monitors the requirements depending on their present stage in the process.

Kanban, on the other hand, is not time-sensitive but rather prioritized. This implies that if a developer wants to move on to the next job, he or she may do so quickly. This method includes a few meetings to aid in planning. It is not the same as Scrum. As a result, it is critical that team members exercise caution. If the developers' pace of work is quicker than the rate of testing in this sort of technique, many bottlenecks will occur. In this instance, any member of the team may join and assist in the various roles.

Kanban offers an easy transition for optimal teams. To achieve an effective and easy transition to Kanban, developers, business analysts, stakeholders, and testers must meet and talk on a frequent basis. When transitioning to Kanban, keep in mind that this type of methodology will provide you with the quickest means of productivity in your code. However, there is a chance that the code contains errors.

Kanban is ideal for small teams or teams that do not create features that should be made public.

Furthermore, it is a high-quality methodology used in various types of products or teams whose primary goal is to keep bugs out of a system.

XP stands for Extreme Programming

Kent Beck is widely regarded as the originator of XP. It is a well-known and contentious agile technique. It focuses on delivering high-quality software in a timely manner. It is based on consumer interaction, immediate input, and subsequent planning and testing.

The XP's basic formula was based on four simple values. Feedback, simplicity, communication, and boldness are among these values. The client collaborates closely with the development team in Extreme Programming. The customer's responsibility is to design and prioritize smaller pieces of functionality known as "User Stories."

To plan and deliver the highest-priority user stories, the development team produces an approximation. These user stories are offered as fully functional and tested applications. To ensure that productivity is maximized, the practices provide a supporting framework that will assist in providing advice to the team.

Crystal

this is by far the lightest and most casual approach. The crystal is made up of a variety of Agile techniques, including crystal orange, crystal yellow, crystal clear, and many more. This Crystal family recognizes that each project may need a unique set of procedures, regulations, and processes. These distinctions contribute to the project's success.

Crystal's measurements include communication, collaboration, and simplicity. Crystal, like other agile techniques, promotes the early and frequent delivery of a functional product. Furthermore, it encourages adaptability, user participation, and the elimination of bureaucracy.

Methodology for the Development of Dynamic Systems

this technique is founded on nine principles that revolve around company requirements, active user involvement, team empowerment, and consistent delivery. DSDM advocates for fitness in the workplace as the primary emphasis in the delivery and adoption of a given system.

The needs are listed early in the project using this process. Processes are improved to make them better.

Iterations of requirements are established and supplied in a short period of time. In the DSDM project, all critical tasks must be completed. Furthermore, not every requirement is given high priority. The DSDM framework is self-contained and must be deployed with other iterative approaches, like XP.

10

Agile Implementation Success Factors

Agile approaches, for example, are difficult to deploy Kanban, Scrum, and many more are examples. As an organization, project manager, and development team, you face several problems. Despite these challenges, the benefits of using agile methodology outweigh the implementation difficulties. Consider the following factors to help you effectively execute an agile approach:

Begin with the proper project.

Agile approaches are ideal for application in any project. However, the type of project determines the most successful implementation. More possibilities are created by starting with the correct project.

Using agile approaches on traditional projects does not provide favorable outcomes. Typically, one may lose control with team members who want to return to old methods. On the other hand, presenting a restricted or highly dynamic scope might be beneficial with agile approaches.

Define the team's role

A team's function while working on a predictive project differs from that of a team working on an agile project. Project managers have complete authority over projects under the conventional approach.

However, in the agile framework, the project manager functions similarly to a driver.

In an agile project, the team must be very disciplined and organized. This is one of the most difficult areas for firms that use management and control methods. Recognizing the necessity of such a team is beneficial. Putting together a cohesive team with the same aim might be the best approach.

It is critical to coordinate activities

the most prevalent issue encountered while applying the Agile approach is the misconception that estimating is unimportant. While project estimates are not required, it is recommended to create one to show when tasks are expected to be completed. This keeps the crew motivated to accomplish the assignment on schedule.

If work is not completed within a particular sprint, there is a probability that the estimate was incorrect and must be rectified. The work must be broken into digestible portions, and the degree of commitment must be updated. Flexible management will guarantee that everyone focuses on the jobs that provide the most value.

Understand and handle your limits

agile approaches have constraints that must be recognized. These include scope, deadline, cost, and quality issues. It is acceptable to negotiate the scope while maintaining time, cost, and quality constraints. These strategies stipulate that a particular job should not exceed a certain level of effort. A timer should also be set up to help make the most of the sprints.

Because limitations are a critical component of the model, it is critical that they remain unchanged or even slightly modified. Any changes may cause one to lose control.

Tension management

certain organizations view agile approaches as a quick way to get things done. However, for these methods to be effective, team tension must be managed. If you can build a team that is motivated, self-managed, results-oriented, and efficient, you will be successful with the Agile technique. Furthermore, in order to see a positive change, each team must cultivate the right attitude toward productivity.

Maintain the technique

agile techniques include a set of norms, regulations, and products. As a result, following the approach properly is essential. It is usually a good idea to leave space for experience by not changing anything. If something unusual occurs, be patient and offer another chance.

Scrum approaches provide a series of phases and meetings that must be followed in order for the methods to function properly. Using these methods, you can progress from less to more. However, the instructions must be followed precisely.

Quality

Quality relates to increasing delivery speed and regulating estimations. When using agile methodologies, it is critical that products are delivered on time. One thing that must be guaranteed is that the things given function. The items must perform what they were designed to accomplish.

As a result, no one should strive to forsake quality throughout the product development process until the ultimate result is achieved.

Keep in mind that power without control is meaningless

these techniques are really effective. They have the power to motivate teams to achieve higher achievements in a shorter period of time. Agile approaches place a strong emphasis on measuring, evaluating, and continuously improving.

Metrics are methods of managing projects that rely on real facts rather than opinions, intuition, or emergencies. Speed, devotion, flow, and compliance are criteria to consider while developing teams and processes.

Improve visibility

this is an important factor in the success of an approach. In some companies, the implementation of these approaches is never made public.

However, it is recommended that this type of implementation be made public so that both the general public and the entire organization can see what is going on.

When the project sponsor arrives, it is critical to avoid employing proprietary Kanban techniques. Gather your courage and present it. Explain and apply the obvious benefits. There is no greater buddy than a project sponsor who becomes active in management. In reality, when working with agile initiatives, this promotes the concept of transparency.

Manage your expectations

most teams and companies that use this strategy assume that their issues will be solved and that the client's perspective will never change. They believe that their products will always be flawless. It is important to recognize that agile approaches do not provide a one-stop solution to all problems. The effectiveness of your technique will be determined by how you handle the numerous demands from management and your staff.

The approach may fail to operate successfully in the first round, making teams uncomfortable with some aspects of the process. This is fairly prevalent and should be taken seriously. Soon, improvement will be seen. This is important, and the outcomes will be beneficial.

Select the appropriate tools

Using support tools to deploy agile techniques increases the likelihood of success throughout the implementation phase

It is critical to establish a centralized support system for sharing information, monitoring progress, and delivering project management.

You should be cautious not to use free tools that are unrelated to your company.

Agile approaches are never applied by teams using amateur tools. It should be the organization's obligation to seek out the appropriate instruments to aid in the adaptation of a particular approach.

Revise and enhance the procedure

Once a methodology has been correctly implemented, the next step is to consider adjustments. Create evaluations that enable you to identify what is and isn't working in your company. These evaluations assist a person in making appropriate changes. However, only do this after you've done some testing with the standard models.

Agile methods are adaptive and versatile. This allows them to be used in a variety of initiatives within a company. With a little practice, one can spot imbalances and react appropriately.

Learn how to be an excellent product owner

a product owner is one of the most crucial people in any agile project and may determine whether the project succeeds or fails. This section examines some of the most common situations that product owners confront in agile contexts.

Understanding and managing stakeholders

Dealing with stakeholders and some of their expectations is one of the most typical issues that product owners face. To be successful in representing stakeholders to developers, the product owner must have total faith and belief in the stakeholder. They must have faith in the product owner and express their requirements to the developers **So, how does one gain the trust of stakeholders?**

The first step is to learn to listen to and learn from stakeholders. If you already know the stakeholders, you have an advantage. However, if you are unfamiliar with them, take the time to become acquainted with them. Begin by introducing yourself, your goals, and your positions. The next step is to ask them questions about their work and requirements. Consider some of their frustrations and hopes for the new solution. People are usually willing to talk about their procedures and offer their degree of knowledge.

There may be times when you will come across critics; these are individuals that do not support the new product and are unwilling to adjust or work for you.

Understand and exert control over the storyboard

the storyboard contains your needs as well as what developers should produce. When the narrative isn't straight or adequately spelled out, the project's prospects of success are slim. As a result, a product owner must concentrate on managing the product backlog and sprints. Feedback from stakeholders should be thoroughly examined. Accept input that is well-defined and has commercial value. The remaining input should either be rejected or investigated. To acquire clean feedback and effective tales, make sure the stakeholders understand what a great narrative and feedback look like. When the project begins, contact the stakeholders and walk them through the process of developing a story and providing feedback. When demonstrating, make a connection between their stories and what the developers have created. As they get more acquainted with and understand the procedure, you should begin to enhance it even more.

Recognize and choose the appropriate product owner

every project, regardless of size, should have several product owners. This will continue to be a struggle, with the possibility of success or failure. Multiple product owners are unlikely to be effective. Why? Making a choice gets challenging. Stakeholders will have a difficult time deciding who to contact. Scrum masters and developers will be unsure to whom they should direct their inquiries. What if there are two conflicting product owners' points of view? Who will be held accountable or become the true owner of the product? Multiple product owners in a project generate assumptions and divergent points of view. Furthermore, it may cause unnecessary confusion when making decisions.

That is why it is critical for each project to have a single product owner. When it comes to selecting the proper product owner, go with someone who is willing to assume complete charge of the whole product and devote the bulk of their time to it. They must understand what should be created and have a clear vision of the ultimate outcome. They should be prepared to communicate with stakeholders and scrum masters. Finally, the ideal product owner prioritizes a project's capabilities and features and conveys the reasoning behind all of his or her choices.

Maintain your cool and automate

A product owner is responsible for managing a large number of individuals and their expectations. This is a substantial amount of work that will require more effort and time. You may experience excessive fatigue at times. It is best to take a break at such times. You may even enlist the help of others. Another thing you can do to be productive is automate communication. The most essential thing is to learn to seek help from upper management when you don't feel comfortable making choices.

Conclusion

Adopting Agile techniques may be the most important shift in the management of the project team. Successful incremental and iterative development requires a project management style that is flexible and progressive. Furthermore, the entire team must embrace the change and the subsequent improvements that this change brings.

To prevent instant opposition to any change, it is critical to convey the relevance of the change. The only way to do this is to produce the correct commercial and technical outcomes in a timely and efficient manner. The easiest method to achieve these goals is to include the modification as part of the task. Iteratively creating agile methods is not difficult. However, changing people's working habits is difficult. This book will provide you with the information you need to execute agile software development processes. Hopefully, the knowledge on agile approaches and methodologies offered in this book can assist anybody in an organization or in the effective completion of a project. Furthermore, using agile best practices will help your organization not only succeed but also thrive.